Secular Divine

Joe Safdie

SPUYTEN DUYVIL
New York City

ACKNOWLEDGMENTS

The author thanks Basil King for the cover illustration,
his painting called "Black 10"
mixed media on canvas / 24 x 30 /
© Basil King, June 2020

The cover page illustration is from
Gustav Dore's illustrations to Dante's *Inferno*: The Heretics

© 2022 Joe Safdie
ISBN 978-1-956005-84-4

THIS BOOK IS DEDICATED TO
the Charles Olson Society,
especially the members of the panel at the Louisville Conference,
Michael Boughn, Patrick Dunagan, and Jeff Davis,
discussions with whom aided the preparation
of these texts immeasurably

Introduction:
The Secular Divine

The essay "Poetry and Heresy: The Secular as Smooth Space" will be included in a larger collection of essays called *Poetry and Heresy* to be published next year by MadHat Press. I thank its editor, Marc Vincenz, for allowing its publication here first, and Tod Thilleman for providing the window. It's accompanied by a suite of poems, "On the Secular," where some of the same ideas are entertained in different forms.

I had originally intended to read the essay at the Louisville Conference in February 2022 as part of a panel called "Olson and the Secular Divine," but the other panelists and I had a small problem: none of us really knew what that meant. One possible clue came from Olson's "Proprioception," where he warned that if we don't see through seven "hinges of civilization" he laid out, "the present will lose what America is the inheritor of: a secularization which not only loses nothing of the divine but by seeing process in reality redeems all idealism fr theocracy or mobocracy." A secularization that stays divine is already complicated, but there are other terms for this confluence that appear throughout his late writing, for example "subterranean and celestial, "Tartaros and Uranos," "geography and etymology" (interestingly enough, from Gertrude Stein), "taxonomic and autonomic," "matter and heaven," and "terrestrial angels."

In this context, one might remember "the absolute condition of present things," a phrase Olson got from Melville, and Corbin's *ta'wil*, which Olson calls "a dipolarity, not a polarization or polarity but a double condition." ("Interview in Gloucester, August 1968"). But laying the terms out this way makes them seem static, forgets his insistence that "the only interest of a spiritual exercise is production" ("Causal Mythology"); a few days later at his Berkeley reading in 1965, he said that he had tried, more than anyone else in our time, to encourage people to believe in their own action.

Jack Clarke, in a letter to Tom Clark, cleared things up a bit: "Point is, as in the Moebius Strip, one side turns into the other easily, and back. And if you don't have or propose the two, what have you got? Certainly not Olson, who was a stickler on this point. Biomorphism, the fusion of the 2 sides into one. He taught, as you know (eg. Last Lectures) always the 2, whether genetics and morphology or etc., but never what Blake accused WW of, the atheism of the world of nature."

This seems a bit like the twin goddesses Demeter and Persephone actually being one deity in the Eleusinian Mysteries. But Michael Boughn, borrowing some terms from Emerson, came up with perhaps the clearest sense of the congruence: "recognition—experience—of a transcendent opposite where transcendent is understood not as out of the world, but as a further dimension of the world, here as folded and unfolded, opening into the surprise of not human, the non-central, an opening beyond the self-enclosure of signification."

As it turned out, the four of us on the panel (Michael, Patrick Dunagan, and Jeff Davis were the others) decided to just have a conversation about Olson rather than read our papers, so "Smooth Space" appears here for the first time. It wouldn't have worked for the panel anyway, as it's more about Edward Dorn and heresy—yet another term for the secular divine—than Olson. As for the poems, they appeared by fits and starts when

I wasn't writing the essay; one of them started on the way to the conference. I hope they gloss the essay, and vice versa, but everyone who writes in hybrid forms hopes that. Mostly, as we continue our brief sojourn through the secular universe, I hope we manage to feel further flashes of the divine.

Portland, April 2022

THE SECULAR DIVINE

Poetry and Heresy:
The Secular as "Smooth Space"

"There must also be heresies among you," warned St. Paul (*I Corinthians* 11:19), recalling the close connection heresy has with orthodoxy; indeed, heresy can only exist when there's an orthodoxy to name it. Such naming kicked into overdrive in the 11th and 12th centuries CE, when the Church defined heresy as "disobedience [to Canon Law] rooted in pride"; as a result, hundreds of those disobedient people were burned at the stake. Dante was a good enough Catholic to consign heretics to Dis, the City of Pain, in the Sixth Circle of Hell.

For Dante, though, heretics' great sin was believing the soul would die with the body, thereby denying God (or, at least, the medieval Catholic god): for him, heretics were heretics because they were secular. Today it seems like a stretch to equate the two terms, but there is a heretical streak in some secular poets, and the two notions are connected in interesting ways. That is, there have always been poets who wrote against the grain of whatever maxims are ascendant at the time, but that's not what I'm talking about here. Edward Dorn's late poem *Languedoc Variorum: A Defense of Heresy & Heretics* comes a little closer—for one thing, his contempt for the Catholic Church is apparent throughout—but while I'll talk a bit about that remarkable work in this essay, it doesn't approach the supreme heresy of a figure like Marguerete Porete, the beguine mystic burned at the stake on June 1, 1310 at the Place de la Grève in Paris (Dante had begun writing the *Commedia* two years before). "There are among us," complained a Franciscan friar in 1274, "women whom we have no idea what to call . . . because they live neither in the world nor out of it." He was talking about women like Porete, who inhabited an ambiguous location between the secular and the religious, and while many spiritual concerns have lost currency today, that location is still on the map: we can see it in the non-Euclidean reality Dorn's teacher Charles Olson wrote about in "Equal, That Is, to the Real Itself" (1958), and it also resembles the "smooth space" of Deleuze and Guattari. Medieval heretics like Porete (as well as her contemporary, Meister Eckhardt) were writing about a place—an attitude, a practice—where the visible and invisible can meet; then as now, the real heresy was experiencing the sacred while still alive.

Deleuze and Guattari introduce "smooth space"—and its opposite, striated space—in *1000 Plateaus* this way: "in the first case space is occupied without being counted, and in the second case, space is counted in order to be occupied."

> Conducive to rhizomatic growth and nomadic movement, smooth space consists of disorganized matter and tends to provoke a sensual or tactical response—haptic—rather than a starkly rational method of operation or a planned trajectory. (477)

This recalls Olson's description of the haptic universe of "Human Universe," where the Mayans "wear their flesh with that difference which the understanding that it is common leads to," and certainly Dorn's *Gunslinger* is one example of space being occupied without "a starkly rational method of operation" (lest we forget, Slinger is the demi-god of "impeccable personal smoothness"). The works I've mentioned constitute an expanded notion of the secular, one that contains its own transcendence and deserves the honorific of heresy.

仝

In the summer of 1958, Olson published the essay "Equal, That Is, to the Real Itself." The occasion was ostensibly a review of a recent book about Melville, but he disposed of the review part quickly: "The idea on which this book is based, naturalism, is useless to cope with Melville." What he really wanted to talk about was the German mathematician Bernhard Riemann, especially his concept of two kinds of manifold, the discrete and the continuous. The continuous was a new concept in the 1850s, which, Olson writes, Melville had unconsciously exploited to write "the first art of space [*Moby Dick*] to arise from the redefinition of the real." Olson identified that art with congruence, or "spatial intuition" (later in the essay, he offered the terms "elliptical and hyperbolic spaces" and "projective space"). In doing so, he drew on quantity, one of the four arcs of study he had laid out to Ed Dorn in the bibliography addressed to him a few years back, but here called it "quantity as intensive" rather than extensive, which made it possible "to get God in the street . . . the necessary secularization of His part in the world of things." This new art of space, Olson wrote, quoting a letter from Melville to Hawthorne, was a way to apprehend "the absolute condition of present things"; indeed, he calls the writing of *Moby Dick* "the only time in a lifetime in which Melville did manage to throw off the Semitic notion of transcendence."

A few years later, in "Proprioception," he described seven different "hinges of civilization" that could be seen by looking at human history through a "continuous" lens, and warned that if we didn't employ it, "the present will lose what America is the inheritor of: a secularization which not only loses nothing of the divine but by seeing process in reality redeems all idealism [from] theocracy or mobocracy." Experiencing the divine without theocracy throws a different light on the voluminous historical records of Gloucester Olson uncovers in *The Maximus Poems*: especially, in *Maximus IV V VI* and the third volume, they're always in the service of the spiritual, whether Hesiod's Greek gods or Corbin's Angels. When those practices are joined by his constant argument against the calcified and traditional academic notions he came across in his reading, it's certainly not a stretch to call him heretical.

I don't know whether the concept of heresy has ever been applied to the ideas of Deleuze and Guattari, but parts of their presentation do resemble Olson's use of the "continuous," for example, "In striated space, lines or trajectories tend to be subordinated to points: one goes from one point to another. In the smooth, it is the opposite: the points are subordinated to the trajectory" (478). And just a few sentences later, there's this:

> In smooth space, the line is therefore a vector, a direction and not a dimension or metric determination. It is a space constructed by local operations involving changes in direction. These changes in direction may be due to the nature of the journey itself, as with the nomads of the archipelagoes (a case of "directed" smooth space), but it is more likely to be due to the variability of the goal or point to be attained, as with the nomads of the desert who head toward local, temporary vegetation (a "nondirected" smooth space). Directed or not, and especially in the latter case, smooth space is directional rather than dimensional or metric. Smooth space is filled by events or haecceities far more than by formed and perceived things. It is a space of affects, more than one

of properties. It is *haptic* rather than optical perception. Whereas the striated forms organize a matter, the smooth materials signal forces and serve as symptoms for them. It is an intensive rather than extensive space, one of distances, not of measures and properties. (478-79)

This is difficult stuff, but it's instructive to note the use of Olson's word "intensive"; also, reading the word "line" here as "poetic line" makes it a pretty close description of Projective Verse. Not only are striated and smooth synonyms for Olson's (and Riemann's) discrete and continuous, they also suggest a secular familiarity with the divine, as in Walter Benjamin's concept of "profane illumination." Indeed, the philosophers caution that the two spaces exist only in mixture: as the conclusion to this chapter states, "Even the most striated city gives rise to smooth spaces: to live in the city as a nomad or as a cave dweller. Movements, speed and slowness, are sometimes enough to reconstruct a smooth space" (499).

A parallel to these ideas can be found in one of our most talented readers of Olson, the poet Don Byrd; in his *Poetics of the Common Knowledge,* he writes that it's possible for people to live "autopoietic lives," propelled by "the proprioceptive equilibrium of their autonomy":

> When it is possible to survey an event in a statistically significant run, science will serve; when we have only one chance, as is always the case for a living being, poetry is required . . . There is also, however, an otherness that cannot be appropriated, an otherness on which we have no hold and that has no hold on us, an otherness that is not a phantom of our own psychic dynamism. Confronted with otherness as utterly alien, the problem of language in all of its originality appears. Discourse, the language that continues by its prearrangements, falls into silence: nothing is *ex*-pressed or *re*-presented. One is required to speak but has no idea what language might be. (337)

Olson had started "Equal, That Is, to the Real Itself" by remembering Keats' notion of negative capability, and this passage by Byrd not only remains in mysteries, uncertainties and doubts but echoes Olson's skepticism of mere "discourse" by invoking a visitation from the Muses (or the Outside, or God), in the face of which, "any *doctrine* [i.e., orthodoxy] must be subsumed by reason, egocentrism . . . The alternatives must issue in a *practice* that can be indicated in a series of injunctions having no authority but their own results" (342). A little later, Byrd summarizes the ideas of the chapter: "The knowledge of nonstatistical probability, Whitehead said, represents 'the secularization of the concept of God's function in the world.' That is, the creation of the world is a secular, fine activity" (348).

소

The connection between this "enhanced secular" and heresy, though, might still be elusive. The word comes from the Greek *hairesis,* "a taking, choice," from the verb *hairein,* "to take." As I mentioned earlier, heresy, in its formal sense in Roman Catholic Canon Law and moral theology, refers to "a sin of one who, having been baptized and retaining the name of Christian, pertinaciously denies or doubts any of the truths that one is under obligation of divine and Catholic faith to believe" writes Lester R. Kurtz in *The Politics of Heresy* (3). For our purposes, it's necessary to remember what heresy meant to Dante:

> He meant an obduracy of the mind; a spiritual state which defied, consciously, a power "to which trust and

obedience are due": an intellectual obstinacy. A heretic, strictly, was a man who knew what he was doing; he accepted the Church, but at the same time he preferred his own judgment to that of the Church. This would seem to be impossible, except that it is apt to happen in all of us after our manner. (125-26)

That's from one of the best books of Dante criticism that I know, Charles Williams' *The Figure of Beatrice,* first published in 1943, and he explains why the idea might seem strange in the next paragraph: Dante, he writes, "believed it to be less important that men should think for themselves than that they should think rightly. We later moderns, on the whole, believe that men had better think for themselves even if they think wrongly" (127).

Of course, the ability to define "thinking rightly" has always been a good gig, and was for the holy fathers. Kurtz identifies some of heresy's more important characteristics:

First, heresy refers to an intense union of both nearness and remoteness. Heretics are within the circle, or within the institution; consequently, they are close enough to be threatening but distant enough to be considered in error . . . The heretic is, furthermore, differentiated from the schismatic or infidel, who is outside the church. When the medieval scholastics developed catalogs of heresies, they were concerned not so much with abstract heresy as with guilty heretics, persons within the community who were defined as a threat to the faith and to the institution . . . Heresy thus has an important social dimension—the heretic is a deviant insider. (3-4)

Edward Dorn has always been identified as a poet (i.e., "within the circle") but could as easily have been called a "deviant insider." Indeed, lots of people wondered about his late practice, and for good reason: he didn't always seem to show the greatest respect for the institution of poetry, as the poem in *Hello, La Jolla* called "Inspection" testifies:

> Poetry is now mostly government product
> therefore we can dispense with the critical apparatus
> the grades assigned to beef will do nicely:
> Prime
> Choice
> Good
> Commercial
> Canners
> Utility

Gunslinger can also be called heretical in the sense that nobody had seen anything like it before; at the very least it shares with heretics a suspicion of the accepted versions of reality. "Someone bumped by the Rational," says the Slinger at the beginning of "The Winterbook" in Book III, "could get on a plea / for unencumbered forward motion." That's mostly because we "are inattentive / and expect reason to Follow / as some future chain gang does / a well worn road" he explains to the narrator in Book 1. Reason may seem like "smooth space," but it's more like what Robart, the villain of this cosmic western, wants to enact in his "Cycle of Acquisition." The real battle, as I wrote in a review of its 50th anniversary publication,

> is between sensate beings, who "wander estranged / through the lanes of the Tenders / of Objects," and those ruled by calculation—those living in space-time or out of it—and that battle is waged, and won, throughout the poem. But it has to be fought again and again, or more precisely, we have to continually re-order our minds and senses and re-orient ourselves so as not to sink into stasis, because Rupert has "only named the game / you know, He AIN'T DELT YET" ("The Cycle," 101).

Avoiding Rupert's plan means to traverse a path where the company becomes "the guest of time / where the afterbirth of space hangs / in the mirror of rime / and where one place / is the center of all this terrific actualism." That passage is from "The Lawg," the short poem that begins the third book, and where a parallel to Deleuze and Guattari's ideas concerning "smooth space" can also be found:

> There is no vacuum in sense
> connection is not by contact
> sense is the only pure time
> connection is a mechanical idea
> nothing touches, connection meant is
> Instant in extent a proposal of limit

For some, the work that came after *Slinger* was a diminution: "The political urgency of the later writing," wrote August Kleinzhaler in a review of *Way More West: New and Selected Poems*, "seems to overtake the poetry and, finally, to undermine it." It was certainly a poetry more based on flat statement than most readers were accustomed to; in a 1977 interview with Stephen Fredman, Dorn read a poem from *Hello La Jolla* and commented

> See, that's exhortatory and pontificatory, you hear that? I was trying for a tone to see how actually flat and rigorously final you could make a line. I think that kind of necessity is left over from a certain bounciness of *Gunslinger* motion. The tone came up as a natural consequence.

He went on to say that he thought he was "done with the La Jolla Book" and didn't feel he needed to follow that rigorous flat style anymore, but he was wrong about that: it was followed by *Yellow Lola* (a series of "outtakes" from *Hello La Jolla* plucked from Dorn's notebooks by Tom Clark in 1980) and *Abhorrences: A Chronicle of the Eighties* (1990), a period of time in which some people questioned whether he was writing poetry at all. He agreed:

> I've been told that an able-bodied person, otherwise in possession of their faculties, really shouldn't do such a childish thing as write poetry. It's hard to ignore that argument. That's why I don't think I write poetry. And

increasingly, I make statements, & if they have the ring of poetry, that's OK—I don't mind.

One of those statements that had the ring of poetry in *Abhorrences* was "The Turk":

> Leading off with a statement
> like "I am Jesus Christ"
> was perhaps a bit strong.
> Nevertheless, if Jesus Christ
> were to return to Earth,
> he'd shoot the Pope.

Rather heretical, even if you don't remember that putative assassination plan in 1983. But after *Abhorrences* was published in 1990, Dorn did, I think, face the dilemma of what else was possible in verse given his predilections and habits of the past 15 years. One attempt was *Westward Haut,* an unfinished poem featuring dogs speaking German on a plane, which didn't quite take off (!), but had some good moments. This is from "Ascending the Platte":

High above the retiring Earth
the final shadows are streaking
the surface, strobing the stubborn tractors
of the breadbasket, illuminating
the resentful faces of their drivers, the groundless
battalions of mechanical serfs—in the airline zines
Land Redistribution is copy long gone,
never to be discussed in the greasy coach
and stopped up toilets of the only venue where
one can see it all—from the still visible impression
of the Oregon trail to the circle compasses, whereby
they have mined the old, untouched waters of the
                                          Aquifer.

"You don't speak German," I said to him once after reading it, and he said "My dogs do." But another work of the nineties, *Languedoc Variorum* (originally called *Languedoc Around the Clock*) is the obvious example of a poem sympathetic to heresy; its subtitle is "A Defense of Heresy & Heretics," and one of the first notes in the vertical middle section of the poem called "Subtexts & Nazdaks" reads "Looking back over the tyranny of Rome and Constantinople, heresy is the only honorable mode and response." There are two poems dedicated to the Japanese gas poisoner Shoko Asahara, who injured 5,500 people "in reprisal for the Americanization of Japan," and one for Ezra Pound, "The Greatest Poet of this expendable century / [who] was also its greatest, most public Heretic."

But *Languedoc Variorum* is also heretical in that it doesn't *look* like anything that came before it: its first 19 pages is made up of three alternating sections, the poems themselves at the top, the "subtexts"—which often give a contemporary gloss to the historical events of the poems—in the middle, and a chyron, or news feed, running across the bottom, which gives an entirely different perspective on "smooth speech." It looks like this:

NAZDAQ PLUNGES, LITERATURE FORCED INTO BANKRUPTCY—BURGHERS OF THEORY REPLACE SAMURAIS OF LITERATURE—MARKET VALUE OF NEW ISSUE NIL—SELL IT—FEAR AND LOAFING UP A NICKLE—WIDEN THE RUNWAY—GOOFBALLS STEADY—TAX SHELTER QUOTATION: INTIMIDATION BY WIELDING THE DEITY LONG TERM—BUY—GROS CHIEN UP HUIT MILLE FRANC—PIG HOCKS GLUT THE MARKET—GET OUT—BODY PIERCING UP A QUARTER—BACTERIA COUNT SHARP INCLINE—VIRUS

BURST STEADY—HOLY VIRGIN UP A NICKLE—FRANCESCA DA RIMINI DOWN FOREVER—FEAR AND LOAFING UP A PESO

Smooth, maybe, but as Deleuze and Guattari write, "smooth spaces are not in themselves liberatory. But the struggle is changed or displaced in them, and life reconstitutes its stakes, confronts new obstacles, invents new paces, switches adversaries." (499-500) These chyrons at the bottom of this poem are a translation of the endless stream of capital, the North Atlantic Turbine that flows through all our interactions, and while some of them are screamingly funny—WESTWARD HAUT—I AM NO GREEK, QUOTED—THE BEARS YAWN—let's be clear: *Languedoc Variorum,* despite its formal eccentricities and collision of language games, is a poem of immense rage. Dorn's contempt for the Inquisition and the corporations that have become its moral equivalent bleeds from every page. Not that this should be surprising: his work from the beginning scorned authority and championed the people crushed under it. Here's the first stanza of a poem from his first book, *The Newly Fallen*, called "Prayers for the People of the World":

> They were an exercise the ages go through
> smiling in the church one time
> banging and blowing in the street another
> where brother is a state very often of glue
> coming apart in the heat
> of British Guiana where
> the drainage and open canals
> make difficult the protection of the lower classes
> who have lands and moneys, food and shelter
> in the great escrow called Never

A brief story: in 1992, while he and his wife Jennifer were in Languedoc, they came to visit my wife and me in the Czech Republic, where we were temporarily living as Peace Corps volunteers (I had managed to get him a reading at the local university). One night in Prague, we met up with other Americans who wanted to eat at an expensive restaurant we couldn't afford, and told them so, but luckily a well-to-do elder diner picked up the check: that didn't prevent Ed's lecturing her on Aristotle's condemnation of usury across the dinner table. He was, as Kleinzhaler put it, "the least endearing, domesticated or predictable of poets, always determined to go his own way, no matter what anyone thought."

But does any of this make him a *heretic*? It's true that his criticism of society is often so severe as to resemble the first heretics, the Gnostics, and their inclination to see the material world as evil. He was also a heretic of sorts in his disgust for official verse culture, his revulsion of mainstream media's "breaking news" and "gangrene crosstalk," and his disdain for anyone who took up a political position: *any* position.

And heresy is finally always a matter of politics. Before Luther, when it arose from religious disputes among Catholics, one of its determinants was social class: for example, Tyndale's translation of the Bible into English, or the lay Beguine movement in France (one of the apostolic groups in Lombardy later persecuted by inquisitorial forces was called The Poor). We know about Dante's association with the White Guelphs and subsequent exile when the Black Guelphs took power; he put his political enemies in his poem not only for reasons of personal spite but because he thought they were tearing the fabric of society—"the community of the faithful"—through their divisive politics. And in these days of insurrection asserted or ignored, it's eerie to re-read one of the epigraphs to *Languedoc Variorum* from Thomas Hobbes: "My country, some few years before the civil wars did rage, was boiling hot with questions concerning the rights of dominion and the obedience due from subjects, the true forerunners of an approaching war."

But I keep coming back to the value of that secular world, where, after all, Porete and other medieval mystics lived and advanced new and different conceptions of what it meant for the divine to meet the human, the state of mind and presence that I'm calling the "secular divine." Here's what Dorn, in that 1977 interview with Fredman, said about the subject:

> There are certain Obligations of the Divine, whether those can be met or not. Part of the function is to be alert to Spirit, and not so much write poetry as to compose the poetry that's constantly written on air. What I've read and what I hear merge to make the field in which I compose.

The etymological history of "secular" gives a few more clues: it's from the Old French *seculer*, from Latin *saeculum* "generation, age," and was used in Christian Latin to mean "the world" (as opposed to the Church). The word was just coming into common usage while Marguerete Porete was alive, c. 1300, and meant something like "living in the world, not belonging to a religious order"; this was extended metaphorically to successive human generations as links in the chain of life. In other words, the medieval "great chain of being" has its roots in the secular.

I started this essay by mentioning Porete, so want to say a little more about her trial for heresy as I close. To the Holy Fathers of the Inquisition, Porete and others like her were "living in the world" a little too much. The main thing that bothered them was her assertion that religious people at a certain level—the fifth station out of seven—could ignore their stringent code of virtues: "a soul annihilated in the love of the creator," she wrote in her book *The Mirror of Simple Souls,* "could, and should, grant to nature all that it desires." But their hyperactive imaginations ignored her subsequent statement that nature "does not demand anything prohibited" of the liberated soul. As Jennifer Deane writes in *A History of Medieval Heresy and Inquisition*,

Virtues, like sins, like will, like the self, are abandoned in the process, all remnants of the distracting and ultimately unreal material realm . . . virtues are no longer necessary *because the liberated soul no longer needs such relatively artificial guides to reach God* (169, her italics).

So, as so often in the centuries of witch-burning to follow, Porete's persecution was a case of lifting passages out of context and interpreting highly metaphoric thought literally. But even though she could have easily defended herself, Porete never uttered a word of explanation or defense in her own behalf. Perhaps she understood, as Michael A. Sells writes in *Mystical Languages of Unsaying,* that "the unrepentant heretic was a defeat for the Inquisition" (141), but better to use her own words to describe "the souls annihilated in love": "They have no shame, no honor, no fear for what is to come. They are secure. Their doors are open. No one can harm them."

Edward Dorn also suffered a metaphorical burning at the stake in his treatment for prostate cancer, which he documented meticulously in his last book, *Chemo Sabe:* "Throat ripping / Ball torching / Fire balling / Gut trenching, war—/ The Iodine drift / In the trenches / The blasting of the seat / of the soul" he wrote in the poem "Iodine Fire." Nevertheless, as he wrote in another poem in that volume, "Tribe," "it would take more paper / Than I'll ever have to express how justified I feel."

On the Secular

there's an Etruscan word, saeculum, *that describes the span of time lived by the oldest person present, sometimes calculated to be about a hundred years. In a looser sense, the word means the expanse of time during which something is in living memory. Every event has its saeculum and then its sunset, when the last person who fought in the Spanish Civil War or the last person who saw the last passenger pigeon is gone.*

                                              Rebecca Solnit

PIE instrumental element
   *-tlo- + *sai- to bind, tie
     (see *sinew*)

the tendon in my finger
   severed   carving knife slips
     clumsily from my hands

the number eight unlocked
   the great chain of being
     revealed as *secular*

"successive human generations
   as links in the chain of life"
     God in the street

making secular
   His part
      in the world of things

仝

driving the freeways
exit ramp off the interchange
around back alleys

requires no particular skill
play it as it lays
past fast food fish joints

shortcuts to the water
if I could find my way
the geography of dream

moving me always north
to the top of the map
where the water is

仝

stretched out on a row of seats
hard black linoleum
empty Atlanta airport
5:30 AM   connecting flight

to Louisville still hours away
to talk about the secular divine
exit rows ain't what they used to be
"that's why they call it a red eye"

mask over my eyes
finally found a use for it
across from a Five Guys
gate drawn shut   red and white squares

early workers get the fryer going
"2018 Readers' Choice:
Voted Best Fries in Dawson"
jazz from someone's cell phone

muzak from the pipes above
Oliver Stone's *Alexander* on the flight
after his Putin interviews
were reshown on Showtime

and a Scheer interview with him
in the morning inbox
Putin invades   traffic jam in Kyiv
harsher sanctions to come

Scheer thought *Alexander* underrated
as it questioned imperial expansion
I thought it mostly sucked
but liked one-eyed Val Kilmer

as Alexander's illegitimate dad
and Angelina Jolie as Grendel's mom
(again)   "reports this morning suggest
Russia has launched a full-scale offensive

in many cities across Ukraine.
Have feedback? Let us know"
6:30 AM   the secular divine
Starbucks 50 feet down the terminal

movement is pleasure
the twisting of an ankle
the body intruding
on the mental landscape
does pleasure need instruction
sips from a thermos
left hand grips right wrist
changing the level of love
waves upon waves
I wrote something like this once
to a coed at UCLA
sitting on the grass
outside the palace
of higher learning

Spiderman on Christmas Eve
three-dee showing
the movie that saved Hollywood

enhanced reality on the menu
from the sea of popcorn on the screen
to the kernels in my palm

the marketing of Meta proceeds
slick formula   gathering
of the three Spider Men

union of three corporations
under the Marvel banner
thick patina of sentiment

this is now The Sacred
everything's last and most forceful assault
on the sanctity of nothingness

Gurdjieff proposed that there are three ways of self-development generally known in esoteric circles. These are the Way of the Fakir, dealing with the physical body, the Way of the Monk, dealing with the emotions, and the Way of the Yogi, dealing with the mind. What is common about the three ways is that they demand complete seclusion from the world. According to Gurdjieff, there is a Fourth Way which does not demand its followers to abandon the world. The work of self-development takes place right in the midst of ordinary life.

Wikipedia

Dore's heretics   Sixth Circle
half in and half out of the grave
carrying death's scent

from the Greek *hairesis*
"a taking, choice"
to make a choice could always

be the wrong choice
it seemed good at the time
but now you're under the earth

in touch with the depths
Tartaros   hidden from the everyday
distant from the mainstream

a world but not that world
autonomic nervous system
similar to dream

not the same as religion
obscuring the simple truth
we're alive because of love

Durkheim's definition of the sacred
that which is "set apart"
removed from the world

because of its connection

with a higher force or being
the Polynesian term *tabu*

meaning "not to be touched"
private property   imperceptible
only the secular common to all
    The Dawn of Everything, Graeber & Wengrow

the day dawns
that's its only task

some people say there's light
at the end of the tunnel
but at the end of that tunnel

is another one
endless and indestructible

isn't that what Williams said?
the day seems like a chance
to forget the night

which waits for all of us
and sometimes accompanies us

during the day

I start breathing again in February
the pagans call it Imbolc
halfway through winter

half the country frozen
paralyzing winter storm
the pagans say spring is coming

Facebook adopts the virtual
shares tumble   biggest wipeout
in market history

income for the quarter only 27 billion
short of expectations
Unbroken Circle   Station Eleven
the possibility of art

reconciling conflicted emotions
it isn't fucking art therapy

Facebook adopts the virtual
all I want is a fucking time machine
"I don't know what I'm going to do"

that feeling's perfect for this scene
family tragedy soothed by narrative
I have found you again   my home

what message did you leave   that I'd
be home soon   I tell them the story
regulate the art market

Roman Law has three basic rights
relating to possession
usus   (the right to use)

fructus (the right to enjoy the products
of a property   the fruit of a tree)
and *abusus*   (the right to damage or destroy)

if one has only the first two rights
it is referred to as *usufruct*
not considered true possession

the defining feature of true legal property
is that one has the option
of *not* taking care of it

even destroying it at will
usufruct nation
secular universe
    The Dawn of Everything, Graeber & Wengrow

Certain philosophers, it is true, taught that the human race was immortal. But we should not underestimate the Greeks' knowledge to the contrary; they knew that whole cities and tribes had perished, on the mainland and on the islands, and that, as Hesiod says earlier, happier races of men had passed away. But nowhere was it stated that those who had perished had been in possession of the Eleusinian rites.

        Carl Kerenyi, Eleusis

仝

today 2 11 22
is the latest solar noon
according to *EarthSky News*

in the morning inbox
not a clock event they add
but natural non statistical

that passing instant when the sun
reaches its highest point for the day
midway between sunrise

and sunset   also 51 days
past the solstice   as Halloween
was 51 days before it

"The Lesser Mysteries took place
in the month of Anthesteria –
falling in mid winter around February

or March . . . to qualify for initiation,
participants would sacrifice a piglet
to Demeter and Persephone" (Wikipedia)

two goddesses become one
divine Eleusis in September
the lesser mysteries

will have to do for now
Ukrainian poets in translation
dismantling the language

syllable by syllable
reading *Maximus* again
Olson wasn't kidding

about an actual earth of value
subterranean and celestial
Saturn and Jupiter

"The conjunction of the two
therefore signifies the union
of extreme opposites" (Butterick)

mythology not a substitute
for what goes on
but there all the same

in the background   what poets turn
these big essential things
aren't going to run away

the poetry of affect
archaic   never political
otherwise it's just art

the meaning of—like, now I can spill it—of tropism in ourselves is the sun. And tropism to my mind—and here I do or again express an experience of say, twenty years ago, which was to me dogmatic, when I knew there was a sun, I mean a helio within myself . . . My feeling is a sun of being which sits in this mass of blackness, or darkness better, or eyelessness or sightlessness, and lends itself . . . the experience of image or vision is as simple as that . . . I mean, obey yourself and in obeying yourself kneel or lean to the sun, or whatever that heliotrope, like, is.

   Olson, "Poetry and Truth"

"mostly cloudy" day on the forecast
still allows a few minutes
of unadulterated sun
a rarity this Portland spring
April is the rainiest month

I like how Robert Kelly's poems
stitch everything together
from the pebbles on the beach
to everyday acts of holiness
wiping tears from a lover's eye

the red flowers that have sprung up
over the last few days
are called Bleeding Hearts—
my wife's health is poor
many tests scheduled   that time of life

Lawrence wrote a story called "Sun"
in which the main character   a woman
has an almost love affair with the sun
the morning started with faint hints
of the miraculous   first leaves

of a skinny ash tree
transplanted Pacific redwood
12 feet high and climbing
an Akhmatova poem posted on Facebook
called "The Miraculous"

she had reason to consider such things
mere privileges for the rich
the treaty of Brest-Litovsk
breast showing through a negligee
objectified in death

Ukrainian poets in translation
witnessing the horror
the language coming apart
syllable by syllable
another day in the secular world

Made in the USA
Middletown, DE
16 July 2022